EMMANUEL JOSEPH

The Neuroscience of Charisma, Unlocking the Brain's Secrets to Captivating an Audience

Copyright © 2025 by Emmanuel Joseph

All rights reserved. No part of this publication may be reproduced, stored or transmitted in any form or by any means, electronic, mechanical, photocopying, recording, scanning, or otherwise without written permission from the publisher. It is illegal to copy this book, post it to a website, or distribute it by any other means without permission.

First edition

This book was professionally typeset on Reedsy. Find out more at reedsy.com

Contents

1	Chapter 1	1
2	Chapter 1: The Essence of Charisma	3
3	Chapter 2: The Charismatic Brain	4
4	Chapter 3: Emotional Resonance	5
5	Chapter 4: Persuasive Power	6
6	Chapter 5: The Science of Attraction	7
7	Chapter 6: Mirroring and Rapport	8
8	Chapter 7: Vocal Charisma	9
9	Chapter 8: Charismatic Leadership	10
10	Chapter 9: Cultural Variations in Charisma	11
11	Chapter 10: Confidence and Charisma	12
12	Chapter 11: Mindfulness and Presence	13
13	Chapter 12: The Journey to Charisma	14
14	Chapter 13: Charisma in Digital Communication	15
15	Chapter 14: The Future of Charisma	17

Chapter 1

Introduction

Charisma, that enigmatic quality that some people seem to naturally possess, has fascinated humans for centuries. It is a magnetism that draws people in, a charm that captivates audiences, and a presence that commands attention. Despite its seemingly magical nature, charisma is not an innate gift bestowed upon a select few. Instead, it is a complex interplay of psychological, social, and neurological factors that can be understood, developed, and harnessed. This book aims to demystify the neuroscience of charisma, providing readers with the tools to unlock their own charismatic potential.

At its core, charisma is a powerful form of communication. It is the ability to convey confidence, warmth, and authenticity in a way that resonates with others. Charismatic individuals excel at making emotional connections, inspiring trust, and motivating action. By examining the brain's role in these processes, we can begin to understand the mechanisms that underpin charismatic behavior. This exploration will reveal that charisma is not a mysterious, intangible quality but rather a skill that can be cultivated through knowledge and practice.

The journey to understanding charisma begins with the brain. Advances in neuroscience have allowed us to map the neural pathways involved in social cognition, emotional regulation, and reward processing. These discoveries have shed light on how certain brain regions, such as the prefrontal cortex and the limbic system, contribute to charismatic behavior. By delving into the brain's inner workings, we can uncover the biological basis of charisma and learn how to enhance our own charismatic abilities.

Emotional intelligence is a key component of charisma. The ability to read and respond to the emotions of others, to express one's own emotions effectively, and to build strong emotional connections is central to charismatic behavior. This book will explore the neural mechanisms of emotional intelligence, highlighting the role of the amygdala and other brain structures in processing and regulating emotions. Practical strategies for developing emotional intelligence will be provided, empowering readers to connect more deeply with those around them.

Charisma is also about the art of persuasion. Charismatic individuals have a unique ability to influence others, to inspire and motivate, and to drive change. This persuasive power is rooted in the brain's reward system, where neurotransmitters like dopamine play a critical role. By understanding the neuroscience of persuasion, readers will gain insights into how to craft compelling messages, engage their audience, and activate the brain's reward pathways. This knowledge will equip readers with the skills to become more persuasive and, ultimately, more charismatic.

This book is your guide to unlocking the brain's secrets to captivating an audience. By blending scientific insights with practical advice, we will embark on a journey to demystify the essence of charisma. Through self-reflection, practice, and a deeper understanding of the brain, readers will learn how to develop and enhance their own charismatic presence, transforming their social interactions and influencing those around them. Welcome to the fascinating world of the neuroscience of charisma.

2

Chapter 1: The Essence of Charisma

Charisma is a magnetic quality that draws people in and holds their attention. It's a blend of confidence, charm, and appeal that makes a person compelling. To understand charisma, we need to look at the traits that make up this elusive quality: confidence, eloquence, empathy, and authenticity.

Historically, charismatic leaders have shaped societies and movements, leaving a lasting impact. This chapter explores these traits and their significance, providing a foundation for understanding the neuroscience behind charisma.

By understanding how these traits interweave to form the fabric of charisma, we can begin to appreciate its complexity. This exploration helps us recognize the conscious and unconscious actions that contribute to a charismatic presence.

The allure of charisma lies in its ability to influence and captivate. Charismatic individuals can navigate social situations with ease, creating a sense of connection and trust. This chapter sets the stage for uncovering the deeper neural mechanisms behind this captivating quality.

3

Chapter 2: The Charismatic Brain

C harisma isn't just a social construct; it has roots in the brain. Specific brain regions, like the prefrontal cortex and the limbic system, play crucial roles in charismatic behavior. The prefrontal cortex governs decision-making and social interactions, while the limbic system manages emotions.

Together, these areas create the behaviors we associate with charisma. By examining these brain regions, we can begin to understand how charisma is neurologically structured.

Recent studies in neuroscience have revealed how neural networks in these regions interact to produce charismatic traits. This understanding opens up new possibilities for enhancing charisma through targeted brain training techniques.

By exploring the neural foundations of charisma, we gain insight into how certain individuals naturally exude charm and confidence. This chapter provides a scientific basis for the charismatic behaviors we observe in everyday life.

4

Chapter 3: Emotional Resonance

A key element of charisma is the ability to resonate emotionally with others. This involves understanding and expressing emotions effectively, a skill known as emotional intelligence. The limbic system, particularly the amygdala, plays a vital role in processing emotions.

Charismatic individuals excel at reading emotional cues and responding appropriately. This chapter delves into the neural mechanisms of emotional intelligence and how it contributes to a charismatic presence.

Emotional resonance is not just about empathy; it's about creating a genuine connection. Charismatic people use their emotional intelligence to build rapport and trust, making their interactions more impactful.

By understanding the neuroscience of emotions, we can develop strategies to enhance our emotional intelligence. This chapter offers practical tips for cultivating emotional resonance and improving our charismatic abilities.

5

Chapter 4: Persuasive Power

Persuasion is a hallmark of charismatic individuals. They have a knack for influencing others and driving decisions. This ability is linked to the brain's reward system, where dopamine plays a significant role. When people are persuaded, their brain's reward pathways are activated, making them more receptive to the message.

Understanding these neural pathways can help us develop techniques to enhance our persuasive abilities and, in turn, our charisma.

Charismatic individuals often use storytelling and emotional appeals to engage their audience. This chapter explores the psychological principles behind effective persuasion and provides practical advice for becoming more persuasive.

The power of persuasion lies in the ability to connect with others on a deeper level. By harnessing the brain's reward system, we can create compelling arguments that resonate with our audience.

Chapter 5: The Science of Attraction

Charisma often includes an element of physical and social attraction. This isn't solely about appearance but also about behaviors that create positive impressions. The brain's mirror neuron system, which is involved in empathy and social understanding, plays a role in this attraction. When we observe charismatic behavior, our mirror neurons fire, creating a sense of connection and attraction.

This chapter explores how these neural processes contribute to the allure of charismatic individuals.

Attraction is a multifaceted phenomenon that involves both conscious and unconscious processes. Charismatic individuals use body language, eye contact, and other nonverbal cues to enhance their attractiveness.

By understanding the science of attraction, we can develop strategies to improve our own charismatic appeal. This chapter provides insights into the neural mechanisms behind attraction and offers practical tips for creating a positive impression.

Chapter 6: Mirroring and Rapport

Building rapport is a critical aspect of charisma, and mirroring is a powerful tool in this process. When we mirror another person's body language, tone, and expressions, we create a sense of trust and understanding. This phenomenon is deeply rooted in the brain's mirror neuron system, which helps us empathize and connect with others.

By honing our mirroring skills, we can enhance our ability to build rapport and be more charismatic. This chapter explores the science behind mirroring, how it fosters connection, and practical exercises for developing this skill. Through conscious practice, we can improve our social interactions and make others feel more comfortable and understood.

Mirroring is not just about imitation; it's about creating a subconscious bond. When done correctly, it can lead to more meaningful and effective communication. This chapter also highlights the importance of subtlety in mirroring, ensuring that it feels natural and not forced.

By understanding the neural basis of mirroring, we gain insight into one of the key tools used by charismatic individuals. This chapter provides a roadmap for mastering the art of mirroring to enhance our social interactions.

8

Chapter 7: Vocal Charisma

The way we use our voice can significantly impact our charisma. Factors such as tone, pitch, and rhythm influence how our message is received. The brain processes these vocal cues in the auditory cortex, and charismatic speakers often have a distinctive vocal style that captivates listeners.

This chapter provides insights into the neural mechanisms of vocal communication and offers practical tips for developing a more charismatic speaking style. We explore techniques for modulating our voice to convey confidence, warmth, and authority.

Vocal charisma is not just about what we say but how we say it. Charismatic individuals use their voice to engage and inspire their audience. This chapter delves into the psychology of vocal communication, offering strategies to make our voice more impactful.

By understanding the neuroscience behind vocal charisma, we can harness the power of our voice to connect with others on a deeper level. This chapter provides practical exercises to refine our vocal skills and enhance our overall charismatic presence.

Chapter 8: Charismatic Leadership

Charisma is a common trait among influential leaders. Charismatic leaders inspire and motivate their followers, often leading to significant social or political change. The brain's prefrontal cortex, responsible for decision-making and social behavior, is crucial in leadership.

This chapter examines the neural basis of charismatic leadership and provides examples of how these principles are applied in real-world scenarios. We explore the traits that make charismatic leaders effective and how they leverage their neural strengths to achieve their goals.

Leadership is not just about authority; it's about creating a vision that others want to follow. Charismatic leaders excel at communicating their vision and rallying people around a common cause. This chapter offers insights into the techniques used by successful leaders to inspire and influence.

By understanding the neuroscience of leadership, we can develop strategies to enhance our own leadership abilities. This chapter provides practical advice for cultivating charismatic leadership skills and making a positive impact on those we lead.

10

Chapter 9: Cultural Variations in Charisma

Charisma is perceived differently across cultures. What is considered charismatic in one culture may not be in another. This chapter explores the cultural differences in charisma, examining how social norms and values influence its expression.

By understanding these cultural nuances, we can better adapt our charismatic behaviors to different social contexts, making our interactions more effective. This chapter highlights the importance of cultural awareness in developing charisma and provides tips for navigating diverse social environments.

Cultural variations in charisma reflect the diverse ways in which people connect and communicate. Charismatic individuals are adept at reading cultural cues and adjusting their behavior accordingly. This chapter offers insights into the skills needed to be charismatic in a globalized world.

By exploring the neuroscience of cultural differences, we gain a deeper understanding of how charisma is shaped by societal norms. This chapter provides practical strategies for enhancing our cross-cultural charisma and building stronger connections in diverse settings.

Chapter 10: Confidence and Charisma

Confidence is a cornerstone of charisma. The brain's reward and fear systems interact to produce confident behavior, which is often perceived as charismatic. Techniques such as positive self-talk, visualization, and resilience training can help build confidence.

This chapter delves into the neuroscience of confidence and offers practical strategies for projecting confidence in social interactions. We explore the brain mechanisms that underlie confident behavior and how we can leverage them to enhance our charisma.

Confidence is not just about self-assurance; it's about how we present ourselves to others. Charismatic individuals exude confidence through their body language, voice, and actions. This chapter provides tips for developing a confident demeanor and overcoming self-doubt.

By understanding the neural basis of confidence, we can develop techniques to boost our self-assurance and charismatic presence. This chapter offers practical exercises to build confidence and make a lasting impression in social interactions.

12

Chapter 11: Mindfulness and Presence

Mindfulness enhances charisma by promoting presence and self-awareness. When we are mindful, we are more attuned to our surroundings and interactions, making us more charismatic. The brain's prefrontal cortex is involved in mindfulness practices, which can improve emotional regulation and reduce stress.

This chapter provides mindfulness techniques that can be incorporated into daily life to enhance charisma. We explore practices such as meditation, deep breathing, and mindful listening, which help us stay present and focused in social interactions.

Mindfulness is not just about relaxation; it's about being fully engaged in the moment. Charismatic individuals are often highly present, making others feel valued and heard. This chapter offers strategies for developing a mindful presence that enhances our interactions and overall charisma.

By understanding the neuroscience of mindfulness, we can leverage these practices to improve our social skills and connect more deeply with others. This chapter provides practical exercises to cultivate mindfulness and boost our charismatic presence.

13

Chapter 12: The Journey to Charisma

Becoming more charismatic is a continuous process of self-improvement and learning. This final chapter offers a roadmap for developing charisma, emphasizing self-reflection, feedback, and practice. We discuss the importance of setting personal goals and tracking progress to enhance our charismatic abilities.

Self-reflection is key to understanding our strengths and areas for improvement. By regularly assessing our interactions and seeking feedback, we can identify ways to enhance our charisma. This chapter provides tools and techniques for effective self-assessment and growth.

Practice is essential in developing charisma. Just as with any skill, the more we practice, the better we become. This chapter offers practical exercises and scenarios to help readers refine their charismatic skills in various social contexts.

The journey to charisma is one of continuous learning and adaptation. By committing to personal growth and applying the techniques discussed in this book, readers can unlock their full charismatic potential and captivate any audience.

14

Chapter 13: Charisma in Digital Communication

In today's digital age, charisma isn't limited to face-to-face interactions; it extends to online communication as well. With the rise of social media, virtual meetings, and digital content creation, understanding how to convey charisma through digital channels is crucial. This chapter explores the unique challenges and opportunities of digital charisma.

Digital communication relies heavily on written text, images, and videos. Unlike in-person interactions, where body language and vocal tone play a significant role, digital charisma must be conveyed through visual and textual cues. This chapter delves into the neuroscience of digital communication, examining how the brain processes and responds to online interactions.

One key aspect of digital charisma is authenticity. Audiences can quickly detect inauthentic behavior online, making it essential to maintain genuine connections. This chapter provides practical tips for building an authentic digital presence, including strategies for effective storytelling, engaging content, and responsive communication.

Another important element of digital charisma is visual appeal. The brain's visual processing centers play a critical role in how we perceive and respond to digital content. This chapter explores the principles of visual design and how they can be used to enhance digital charisma. From creating eye-catching graphics to utilizing color psychology, readers will learn how to captivate their online audience.

By understanding the neuroscience of digital communication, readers can develop strategies to enhance their online charisma. This chapter offers practical exercises and tips for creating a charismatic digital presence, helping readers stand out in the crowded online landscape.

15

Chapter 14: The Future of Charisma

As we continue to explore the neuroscience of charisma, it's important to consider how this knowledge will shape the future. Advances in technology, neuroscience, and social dynamics will influence how we understand and develop charisma. This chapter looks ahead to the future of charisma and its implications for personal and professional growth.

One area of interest is the potential for brain training and neurofeedback to enhance charismatic traits. Emerging technologies that allow us to monitor and influence brain activity could offer new ways to develop charisma. This chapter explores the possibilities and ethical considerations of using neuroscience-based tools for personal development.

The future of charisma also involves adapting to changing social norms and cultural shifts. As societies evolve, so do the traits and behaviors considered charismatic. This chapter examines how global trends, such as increased connectivity and cultural diversity, will impact the expression and perception of charisma.

Additionally, the rise of artificial intelligence and virtual reality presents new opportunities for studying and enhancing charisma. AI-driven virtual environments can simulate social interactions, providing a safe space for practicing charismatic behaviors. This chapter discusses the potential benefits and challenges of integrating AI and VR into charisma development.

Ultimately, the future of charisma lies in our ability to continuously learn and adapt. By staying informed about the latest scientific discoveries and technological advancements, readers can remain at the forefront of charismatic development. This chapter offers a forward-looking perspective on the evolution of charisma and encourages readers to embrace the ongoing journey of personal growth.

The Neuroscience of Charisma: Unlocking the Brain's Secrets to Captivating an Audience

Have you ever wondered what makes certain individuals irresistibly captivating? How do some people effortlessly command attention, inspire trust, and motivate action? In "The Neuroscience of Charisma," we delve into the fascinating world of charisma through the lens of neuroscience, revealing the secrets behind this elusive quality.

Charisma isn't just an enigmatic charm; it's a blend of psychological, social, and neurological factors that can be understood and developed. This book breaks down the components of charisma, from emotional intelligence and persuasive power to vocal charisma and confident behavior, and examines their roots in the brain. By exploring the neural pathways involved in social cognition, emotional regulation, and reward processing, readers will gain scientific insights into the foundations of charismatic behavior.

Each chapter offers a deep dive into specific aspects of charisma, providing practical tips and exercises for readers to enhance their own charismatic presence. From understanding the role of mirror neurons in building rapport to leveraging the brain's reward system for persuasive communication, this book equips readers with the knowledge and tools to unlock their full charismatic potential.

"The Neuroscience of Charisma" also addresses the challenges and opportunities of digital charisma, cultural variations in charismatic behavior, and the future of charisma in a rapidly evolving world. By blending cutting-edge neuroscience with practical advice, this book is a comprehensive guide for anyone looking to captivate an audience and make a lasting impact.

Embark on this journey of self-improvement and discover how to harness the power of your brain to become more charismatic and influential. Whether you're a leader, a communicator, or simply someone looking to enhance

CHAPTER 14: THE FUTURE OF CHARISMA

your social skills, "The Neuroscience of Charisma" provides the roadmap to unlocking your inner charm.

www.ingramcontent.com/pod-product-compliance
Lightning Source LLC
LaVergne TN
LVHW020509080526
838202LV00057B/6266